AS IS

3 TONY AWARD NOMINATIONS

"Powerful, disturbing, extraordinary."
Jack Kroll, *Newsweek*

"A moving work filled with wry humor rather than self-pity . . . exceptionally honest . . . filled with dignity. In many ways *As Is* is a collage of the whole fearsome climate this lethal disease has created in its wake . . . *As Is* gives audiences not only something to shudder over but think about as well."
William A. Raidy, *The New Jersey Star Ledger*

"One of the best plays of the season. A remarkable and rewarding evening of theatre."
Judith Crist, WOR-TV

"Unforgettable! The best of theater!"
Joanna Langfield, ABC Radio

"The most impressive work on or off Broadway."
Variety

"Written with passion and purpose. You leave the theatre shaken!"
Joel Siegel, ABC-TV

"Deeply affecting and very funny."
William A. Henry III, *Time*

AS IS

A Play by

William M. Hoffman

Random House
New York

First Vintage Books Edition, October 1985
 Published in the United States by Random House, Inc., New York, and simultaneously in Canada by Random House of Canada Limited, Toronto. Hardcover edition published simultaneously by Random House, Inc.

Manufactured in the United States of America
Cover art courtesy © 1985 Fraver

In memory of:

R. A.
Fortunato Arico
Stephen Buker
Gregory Y. Connell
Wilfredo Davilla
Tom Ellis
Timothy Farrell
George Harris
Pierre Murue
Arthur Naftal
Giulio Sorrentino
Larry Stanton
Larry Waurin
Stuart White

The "Red Death" had long devastated the country. No pestilence had ever been so fatal, or so hideous. . . . The scarlet stains upon the body . . . were the pest ban which shut the victim out from the sympathy of his fellowmen. . . . But the Prince Prospero was happy and dauntless and sagacious. When his dominions were half depopulated, he summoned to his presence a thousand hale and light-hearted friends . . . and with these retired to the deep seclusion of one of his castellated abbeys. . . . A strong and lofty wall girdled it in. The wall had gates of iron. The courtiers brought furnaces and massy hammers and welded the bolts. . . . With such precautions the courtiers might bid defiance to contagion. In the meantime it was folly to grieve, or to think. The Prince had provided all the appliances of pleasure. There were buffoons, there were improvisatori, there were ballet-dancers, there were musicians, there was Beauty, there was wine. All these and security were within. Without was the "Red Death."

—Edgar Allan Poe, *The Masque of the Red Death*

My tale was heard, and yet it was not told;
My fruit is fallen, and yet my leaves are green;
My youth is spent, and yet I am not old;
I saw the world, and yet I was not seen;
My thread is cut, and yet it is not spun;
And now I live, and now my life is done.

—Chidiock Tichborne, "Elegy"

Special Thanks

Jerry Vezzuso

Beth Allen, Nestor Almendros, John Bishop, George Boyd, Victor Bumbalo, John Corigliano, David Courier, Penny Dashinger, Barry Davidson, East End Gay Organization, Gay Men's Health Crisis, Barbara Grandé-LeVine, Jay Harris, Stephen Harvey, Joel Honig, Reed Jones, Daniel Irvine, David Kapihe, Robert Kubera, Rodger McFarland, Terrence McNally, Barbara Myers, Claris Nelson, Constance Mary O'Toole, Kent Paul, Candida Scott Piel, David Richardson, Luis Sanjurjo, Mary Scarborough, June Stein, Paul Theobald, Dr. Kenneth Unger, Tobin Wheeler, Lanford Wilson, the New York Foundation for the Arts for their generous support, and

Marshall W. Mason

AS IT WAS

"It must be the combination of quiche and leather," I think I joked to a friend over the phone the first time I heard about the mysterious new disease attacking gay men. It was 1980, '81, I'm not sure. I think it was early spring and I was sitting in my office, drinking my first decaffeinated espresso of the morning. I had just finished reading the previous day's *New York Times.* I like to have my news a little stale so I don't get too alarmed at the state of the world. I told my friend the article was absurd: a disease capable of distinguishing between homo- and heterosexual men? Come on.

At the time, I was in the midst of writing Act One of the libretto to *A Figaro for Antonia,* which the Metropolitan Opera had commissioned, and when I wasn't writing I was jogging. So, for a period, I was totally immersed in work. When I came back up for air it registered that my roommate's best friend, Tim, was dying in a hospital in San Francisco. He had a pneumonia that antibiotics couldn't touch, and wild viral infections of the brain. He finally fell into a coma and succumbed.

But was it really surprising, I asked myself, that Tim would get ill? A terrific person, generous, funny, warm, but definitely in the fast lane. And when Freddy went into the hospital I told myself that he had been looking for trouble: I mean, he practically lived at the gay bathhouses. People like me were not going to come down with AIDS. I wasn't going to the baths. I didn't drink or take drugs. And I was running twenty to thirty miles a week. I felt invulnerable.

And then Larry took sick: mild ailments that wouldn't clear up, not bothersome enough to stop him from running the marathon faster than I could conceive of doing. Larry was younger than I, and he didn't drink or take drugs. A few months later he died.

And then Brian, who lived over in the East Village. And then George, the kid from the early Caffe Cino days of Off-Off-Broadway. And then Freddy the cellist. And then that guy who ran the flower shop on Sixth—what was his name?

I was busy writing a comic opera as daily the news got worse. My close friend Stephen came down with a chronic case of swollen glands, which was labeled an "AIDS-related complex." It seemed as if the disease were closing in on me personally. I was reminded of the pre–Salk vaccine polio epidemic of my childhood, when you avoided movie theaters and swimming pools. I remembered Wally, the boy upstairs who liked to bully me, until infantile paralysis made him weak and stupid, and I remembered classmates who suddenly stopped coming to school.

But during the polio epidemic, as during the Tylenol and Legionnaire's disease scares, the media and the government committed themselves wholeheartedly to the side of the victims. In the early eighties, with few exceptions, the main concern of people outside the gay community was reassuring themselves that it was happening only to "them," and not to "us." I felt isolated from society in a way I never had before.

As the mortality figures mounted, and as I heard stories of people with AIDS being abandoned by friends and families, mistreated by health workers, and evicted from apartments (in one case being thrown from a window), stories of the Holocaust came to my mind. Most of my family in Europe had perished during the war. As far as I know they never made it to the concentration camps, but were murdered on the street by their Polish and Latvian neighbors. I knew intellectually that the epidemic was *not* the Holocaust, but I had no other experience of mass death and public indifference and brutality to compare it with.

I was writing about the rebellion of Figaro and the tragedy of Marie Antoinette when I learned that my favorite uncle, Wolf, had cancer. And my father was not recovering from his stroke as fully as I had hoped. All around me there was illness and death. I fell into a depression.

So, sometime in 1982, as a sort of a therapy, I started to express my feelings on paper. I decided to write a play about a man named Rich—a writer and runner—who comes down with AIDS; his former lover, Saul; and their friends and families.

I did my research. I visited friends who had the disease; I talked with a hospice worker; I went to support groups; I attended lectures; I made field trips to the Gay Men's Health Crisis (the most important organization dealing with the disease in New York City); I spent hours eavesdropping in gay bars, taking the public pulse.

I was willing to go to any lengths for my play, except to imagine myself having AIDS. I was not afraid of contracting the disease through casual physical contact with those who had it. I was well aware that AIDS is transmitted only by an exchange of body fluids. But on a deep irrational level, I was terrified of catching it by identifying with those who had it.

Consequently, for a long period, my central characters, Rich and Saul, were shadowy and undeveloped, compared with the background figures. But one day I realized the depth of my fear and asked God to protect me as I wrote the play. He did.

All along my characters cracked jokes, which I tried to suppress. People were in the process of expiring, and here I was laughing. I mean, this was supposed to be a *serious* play. Well, I had to do something to keep my spirits up, I rationalized.

Half hoping to depress myself, I'd call up my uncle, and to my chagrin he'd make me smile with some reminiscence of the Yiddish theater. (He was a playwright and poet, like me.) And my father was always eager for a joke, the dirtier the better—and he was in his eighties.

I was having dinner with my friend Constance Mary O'Toole, who was a hospice worker at St. Vincent's Hospital in Greenwich Village, in the heart of New York's gay community, when it finally dawned on me that maybe humor was a key to my play. She said, "We tell a lot of jokes in my line of work." I also began to realize that among the people with AIDS that I was meeting, those with a sense of humor were doing better than those without.

I permitted the play to be funny. I found that audiences at the Circle Repertory Company, where I was workshopping sections of the piece as I wrote them, responded to the humor. It enabled them to accept the pain of the sadder material.

Encouraged by my director, Marshall W. Mason, and producer John Glines, I also allowed the spirit of *A Figaro for Antonia* to infiltrate *As Is.* I asked myself, "Why should I write a totally realistic play, when I take extravagant liberties with time and space in musical theater? Why can't I allow my characters to speak eloquently, when I'm planning to let them do that at the Met?"

By the time we moved from our Off-Broadway home at the Circle Rep to the Lyceum Theater on Broadway, the good humor and the good spirits of some of the people with AIDS that I had met, their lovers and families, people like Connie O'Toole, and my family (my father and uncle died in 1984) had completely subverted the depression that prompted the writing of the play.

Facing my own worst fears has made me feel . . . What do I feel now? Sad at the loss of friends. Frustrated by my powerlessness over a force of nature. Angry at those who have the power to help and won't. But I'm pretty comfortable with people who have AIDS. I'm sane on the subject of my own health. And when I'm frightened in this time of trouble, I'm loving to myself.

AS IS *was developed in the Circle Repertory Company Lab's playwrighting and directing workshops under the leadership of Daniel Irvine. It was directed by George Boyd.*

AS IS *was first presented by the Circle Repertory Company and The Glines, at the Circle Repertory Company, New York City, March 10, 1985.*

The play opened at the Lyceum Theatre, May 1, 1985. It was produced by John Glines/Lawrence Lane, Lucille Lortel, and The Shubert Organization (associate producer Paul A. Kaplan).

The cast, in order of appearance, for both productions:

HOSPICE WORKER	Claris Erickson
RICH	Jonathan Hogan
SAUL	Jonathan Hadary
CHET	Steven Gregan
LILY	Lily Knight
BROTHER	Ken Kliban
BUSINESS PARTNER	Claris Erickson
PICKUP 1	Ken Kliban
PICKUP 2	Lou Liberatore
CLONE 1	Mark Myers
CLONE 2	Lou Liberatore
CLONE 3	Steven Gregan
BARTENDER	Ken Kliban
MARTY	Mark Myers
VINNIE	Steven Gregan
PWA 1	Mark Myers
PWA 2	Lily Knight
PWA 3	Ken Kliban

PWA 4	Lou Liberatore
PAT	Lou Liberatore
BARNEY	Ken Kliban
NURSE	Claris Erickson
HOSPITAL WORKER	Lou Liberatore

Also: Doctors, TV Announcer (Prerecorded), Average People, Drug Dealers and Customers

Directed by Marshall W. Mason
Settings by David Potts
Lighting by Dennis Parichy
Costumes by Michael Warren Powell
Sound by Chuck London Media/Stewart Warner
Production Stage Manager Fred Reinglas

Characters

SAUL
RICH

Four other men and two women play the following:

HOSPICE WORKER
CHET
BROTHER
BUSINESS PARTNER
LILY
TV ANNOUNCER (Prerecorded)
DOCTORS (5)
BARTENDER
PICKUPS (2)
MARTY
VINNIE
CLONES (3)
PEOPLE WITH AIDS (4)
AVERAGE PEOPLE (6)
HOTLINE COUNSELORS (2)
NURSE
HOSPITAL WORKER
DRUG DEALERS AND CUSTOMERS (5)

Set

The play is set in New York City in the present.

Stage right is SAUL*'s fashionable loft space, suggested by a sofa, Barcelona chair, bench, and area rug. Upstage center is a bar, stage left, a bench.*

Except for short exits, the actors remain onstage for the whole play. There is no intermission.

Production Note

In approaching the original production of *As Is,* I felt it was important to find a visual stage life for the play that permitted the freedom of time and place that the text suggests. David Potts, the designer, and I came up with an open stage that suggested simultaneously the stature of the classical Greek theater and the frankness of Brecht, and still allowed the audience, with a little imagination, to see the realistic studio/apartment of a New York photographer. I feel it is important that the actors remain on stage as much as possible, to witness as a community the events of the play in which they do not participate as characters. The audience must be kept from feeling "safe" from this subject, so the actors of the "chorus" must act as a bridge between the fictional characters and the real theater event, and also as an unconventional kind of "threat"—keeping the audience aware that entertaining as the play may be, the subject is deadly. The desired effect is to assist the audience in a catharsis, as they are required to contemplate our common mortality.

—*Marshall W. Mason*

The HOSPICE WORKER, *a dowdy middle-aged woman wearing a dark dress and bright lipstick and nail polish, walks downstage center and addresses the audience.*

HOSPICE WORKER Mother Superior always used to say, "Watch out for the religious cranks, Sister Veronica." When I started working for the hospice I had a touch of the crank about me. I think maybe that's why they gave me the old heave-ho from the convent. But I've kept my vow of chastity and I've made a pilgrimage to Lourdes.

My job is to ease the way for those who are dying. I've done this for the last couple of years. I work mainly here at St. Vincent's. During the day I have a boring secretarial job, which is how I support my career as a saint.

I was much more idealistic when I started. I had just left the convent. I guess I thought working with the dying would give me spiritual gold stars. I thought I'd be able to impart my great wisdom to those in need of improvement. I wanted to bear witness to dramatic deathbed conversions, see shafts of light emanating from heaven, multicolored auras hovering above the heads of those in the process of expiring. I always imagined they would go out expressing their gratitude for all I had done.

A quick joke: Did you hear about the man who lost his left side? . . . He's all *right* now. All right now. *(She laughs)* We tell a lot of jokes in my line of work.

(She takes her seat. Lights come up on two casually dressed men around thirty seated in the living area)

RICH You take Henry.

SAUL Cut him in half.

RICH You can keep him.

SAUL What are we going to do about him?

RICH I said he's yours.

SAUL You found him.

RICH I don't want him.

SAUL Chet doesn't like cats?

RICH I knew this would happen. Don't start in.

SAUL We gotta get things settled.

RICH Then let's. How 'bout if we simplify things: sell everything and split the cash.

SAUL Even the cobalt glass?

RICH Yes.

SAUL And Aunt Billie's hooked rug? Say, how's she doing?

RICH She's on medication. Sell the rug.

SAUL I will not sell the manikin heads. I don't care what you say.

RICH Then take them.

SAUL And the chromium lamp? I love that lamp.

RICH Take it.

SAUL And the Barcelona chair?

RICH The Barcelona chair is *mine! (Beat)* Fuck it. Take it. Take everything. I won't be Jewish about it.
(He rises to go)

SAUL Why didn't you warn me we were going to play Christians and Jews today? I would have worn my yellow star.

RICH I've gotta go.
(RICH *is leaving)*

SAUL Where're you going?

RICH I'm not feeling so hot. Let's make it another day.

SAUL *(Blocking his way)* Sit down.

RICH *(Pushing his hand away)* Don't push me.

SAUL Sorry. I don't like this any more than you, but we gotta do it. It's been six months. *(He lightens things up)* A divorce is not final until the property settlement.

RICH Saul . . . ?
(He's about to say something important)

SAUL What, Rich? *(He waits expectantly)* What?

RICH Never mind.

SAUL What? . . . What? . . . You always do that!

RICH I want the chair.

SAUL You can have the fucking Barcelona chair if Chet wants it so bad! . . . What about the paintings? Do you want to sell the Paul Cadmus?

RICH Yes.

SAUL You love the Cadmus. *(Silence)* And who's going to buy the Burgess drawings? Did you hear that Kenny had a heart attack?

RICH We'll donate them to the Met.

SAUL Just what they always wanted: the world's largest collection of Magic Marker hustler portraits.
(RICH *nods)*

RICH They're yours.

SAUL But you commissioned them. We'll split them up: I get the blonds and you get the blacks—or vice versa.

RICH All yours.

SAUL Then you get the Mickey Mouse collection.

RICH Sell it.

SAUL You don't sell collectibles. Not right now. What's with this money mania? Between the book and the catering, I thought you were doing well.

RICH I want to build a swimming pool.

SAUL You don't swim.

RICH I want a Mercedes.

SAUL You don't drive. It's Chet—he'll bankrupt you! *(Beat)* I don't believe I said that . . . *(He speaks sincerely)* Your book is beautiful.

RICH I never thanked you for the cover photograph.

SAUL *(Shrugging off the compliment)* How's it selling?

RICH Not bad—for short stories. Everyone mentions your photo. Ed White said—

SAUL Your book is terrific. Really.

RICH I'm glad you like it.

SAUL One minor thing.

RICH What's that?

SAUL I thought the dedication was a bit much.

RICH Why are you doing this?

SAUL Don't you think quoting Cavafy in Greek is a little coy?

RICH Please!

SAUL Why didn't you just say, "To Chet, whose beautiful buns inspired these tales"?

RICH Jesus!

SAUL I'm sorry!
(Silence)

RICH I sold the Krugerrands. You were right about them. You have always been right about money. *(He hands* SAUL *a check)* This includes the thousand I borrowed for the periodontist.

SAUL You sure?

RICH Take it.

SAUL I'm not desperate for it.

RICH It's yours.

SAUL I don't want it.

RICH Damn it!

SAUL *(Taking the check)* Okay.

RICH That makes us even now.

SAUL *(Examining the check)* Clouds and trees.

RICH Let's get on with this.

SAUL Is he waiting for you downstairs? You could have told him to come up.

RICH Shit. No! Can it. *(Beat)* I won't be wanting the copper pots.

SAUL Why not? When you and Chet move to your space you'll want to cook again.

RICH I just don't want them! People change. *(Silence)* I'm eating out a lot.

SAUL Chet can't cook?

RICH *(Deciding not to respond with a bitchy comment)* You keep the rowing machine.

SAUL Have you lost weight?

RICH And the trampoline.

SAUL There's some Black Forest cake in the fridge. (SAUL *goes toward the kitchen to get the cake)*

RICH Stop it.

SAUL Stop what?

RICH Just stop.

SAUL I can't.

RICH We're almost through.

SAUL I have feelings.

RICH You have only one feeling.

SAUL He won't make you happy.

RICH Here we go again. (RICH *gets up to go)*

SAUL Don't!

RICH Keep everything.

SAUL I'm not myself.

RICH Nothing is worth this.

SAUL I've been upset.

RICH I mean it.

SAUL Don't go. Please. (RICH *sits. There is a long pause)* I visited Teddy today at St. Vincent's. It's very depressing . . . He's lying there in bed, out of it. He's been out of it since the time we saw him. He's not in any pain, snorting his imaginary cocaine, doing his poppers. Sometimes he's washing his mother's floor, and he's speaking to her in Spanish. Sometimes he's having sex. You can see him having sex right in front of you. He doesn't even know you're there. *(Pause. Both men look down at their feet)*

Jimmy died, as you must have heard. I went out to San Francisco to be with him the last few weeks. You must have heard that, too. He was in a coma for a month. Everybody wanted to pull the plug, but they were afraid of legal complications. I held his hand. He couldn't talk, but I could see his eyelids flutter. I swear he knew I was with him. *(Pause)*

Harry has K.S., and Matt has the swollen glands. He went in for tests today . . . I haven't slept well for weeks. Every morning I examine my body for swellings, marks. I'm terrified of every pimple, every rash. If I cough I think of Teddy. I wish he would die. He *is* dead. He might as well be. Why can't he die? I feel the disease closing in on me. All my activities are life and death. Keep up my Blue Cross. Up my reps. Eat my vegetables.

Sometimes I'm so scared I go back on my resolutions: I drink too much, and I smoke a joint, and I find myself at the bars and clubs, where I stand around and watch. They remind me of accounts of Europe during the Black Plague: coupling in the dark, dancing till you drop. The New Wave is the corpse look. I'm very frightened and I miss you. Say something, damn it.

(Beat)

RICH I have it.

(Immediately, the lights come up on the left side of the stage)

CHET *(A handsome, boyish man in his early twenties)* You what?

LILY *(A beautiful woman, thirtyish)* You have what?

BROTHER *(To his wife, whom we don't see)* He has AIDS.

SAUL I don't think that's funny.

BUSINESS PARTNER The idea is ridiculous.

RICH That's the bad news.

PARTNER You ran the goddamned marathon.

LILY Darling!

RICH The good news is that I have only the swollen glands.

(Two doctors in white gowns appear)

DOCTOR 1 We call it a "Pre-AIDS Condition."

DOCTOR 2 "AIDS-related Complex."

RICH And I've lost some weight.

SAUL I'm in a state of shock.

LILY Move in with me. Chet doesn't know how to take care of you.

RICH I tire easily. My temperature goes up and down.

DOCTOR 1 Your suppressor cells outnumber your helper cells.

BROTHER I don't care what he has, Betty, he's my brother.

CHET You're my lover.

LILY You're my buddy.

PARTNER Rich and I started the business about a year ago. But now word got out that Rich has this disease. I tried to explain: he doesn't touch the food; I do all the cooking. But they won't listen.

BROTHER I'm not in the habit of kissing my brother. I touched him on the back when I arrived and when I left.

PARTNER Why would they? I wonder if I'd use a caterer who had AIDS.

SAUL Doctors make mistakes all the time.

DOCTOR 2 There are a number of highly experimental treatments.

DOCTOR 1 Of highly experimental treatments.

CHET If you don't mind, I'll sleep on the couch tonight. You've been sweating a lot.

LILY I can't turn it down. The work is shit, and who wants to tour Canada in January, but they're paying me a fortune.

BROTHER When he offered me a cup of coffee I told him I'd have a can of beer.

LILY I'll be back in four weeks.

PARTNER I can understand what he's going through. Myself, I've been wrestling with cancer for a while.

SAUL Remember when they told my niece she had skin cancer? It turned out to be dry skin.

I'm winning.

CHET I hope you don't mind, but I'll use the red soap dish and you'll use the blue.

RICH Christ! I've been putting the blocks to you nightly for months and now you're worried about sharing the fucking soap dish?

BROTHER Christ, I didn't even use the bathroom, even though I had to take a leak so bad I could taste it. Now, that's paranoid.

PARTNER I wonder if it's safe to use the same telephone, or whether I'm being paranoid.

CHET I know I'm being paranoid.

LILY They're flying me out to the Coast. I hate that place.

RICH Chet, you've been out every night this week. Do you have to go out again?

BROTHER I know you're scared, Betty, but I will not tell my own brother he's not welcome in my house.

CHET Need something from outside?

BROTHER He's spent every Christmas with us since we got married, and this year will be no exception.

RICH Forget I said anything: just don't wake me up when you get in.

BROTHER You're forcing me to choose between you and my brother.

CHET See you later.

LILY I've been dating this guy—can you imagine *me* dating? Well, he's very nice, and he's got a lot of money, and he's not impressed with my life in the theater—and that's why I haven't been up to see you. Rich?

CHET You know I'd do anything for you.

RICH You're walking out on me.

BROTHER We're going to Betty's mother for Christmas.

CHET I need more space to get my head together.

SAUL What did you expect?

RICH Chet, please, I need you!
(RICH *tries to put his arms around* CHET. *Everyone except* SAUL *pulls back terrified)*

CHET, BROTHER, LILY, PARTNER, DOCTORS *Don't touch me!*
(Beat)

LILY Please forgive me!

CHET This thing has me blown away.

BROTHER If it weren't for the kids.

PARTNER I don't know what the hell we're going to do.

SAUL Bastards!

(CHET, BROTHER, PARTNER, LILY *put on white gowns and become doctors)*

RICH *(To* DOCTOR 1) Doctor, tell me the truth. What are my chances?

DOCTOR 1 I don't know.

RICH *(To* DOCTOR 2) Doctor, tell me the truth. What are my chances?

DOCTOR 2 I don't know.

RICH *(To* DOCTOR 3) What are my chances?

DOCTOR 3 I just don't know.

RICH *(To* DOCTORS 4 *and* 5) Am I going to make it, doctors, yes or no?!

DOCTORS 4 AND 5 I'm sorry, we just don't know.

SAUL Rich?

DOCTORS We don't know.

TV ANNOUNCER *(Prerecorded)* The simple fact is that we know very little about Acquired Immune Deficiency Syndrome. Its victims may live a normal life span, or they may have only a few weeks. Fortunately, so far this tragic disease has not spread outside its target groups to people like you and me. When will science conquer this dreaded plague? We don't know. We don't know. We simply don't know. Don't know . . .

SAUL And for three months you kept this from me. *(The* DOCTORS *exit. We're back in* SAUL*'s apartment)*

RICH I don't want your pity.

SAUL You're my friend. You'll stay with me till you feel better.

RICH Aren't you afraid I'll infect you?

SAUL Yes, I'm afraid.

RICH Paper plates, Lysol, face masks—no, I'd prefer to live alone, thank you.

SAUL You need me.

RICH Besides, if I live with you, where am I going to bring my tricks?

SAUL You pick up people?

RICH *(Standing at the bar)* I go to bars . . . I pick up guys . . . but I give them a medical report before we leave . . . *(Without a pause, we're in a bar.* RICH *is talking to a stranger)* I should tell you something.

PICKUP 1 You like something kinky. Whips? Golden showers? Fist?

RICH It's not like that.

PICKUP 1 I once picked up a guy liked to be yelled at in German. The only German I know is the "Ode to Joy" from Beethoven's Ninth. *(He yells like an enraged Nazi)* "O Freude, schöner Götterfunken, Schweinehund, Tochter aus Elysium, Dummkopf!"

RICH I have a very mild case of lymphadenopathy.

PICKUP 1 What's that?

RICH An AIDS-related condition.

PICKUP 1 Oh, shit.

RICH Just the swollen glands—

PICKUP 1 No way. Uh-uh . . . Good luck . . . Oh, man . . .

(PICKUP 1 *exits. We're back with* RICH *and* SAUL)

RICH So I stopped telling them.

SAUL You mean you take them home and don't tell them?

RICH We do it there in the bar.

SAUL How can you?

RICH I lurk in dark corners where they can't see my lumps. I'm like a shark or a barracuda, and I snap them up and infect them.

SAUL How can you joke about this?

RICH I don't care. I'm going to die! I'll take as many as I can with me. And I've pissed in the Croton Reservoir. I'm going to infect the whole fucking city! Wheeeee!

SAUL No fucking around, give me a straight answer. Do you still pick up people?

RICH Maybe I ought to wear a sign around my neck and ring a bell: "AIDS, I've got AIDS, stand clear!" Would that make you happy? Or maybe I should dig a hole in the ground, douse myself with kerosene, and have a final cigarette. No muss, no fuss. Is that what you want?

SAUL Forgive me for not trusting you. It's just that I'm frightened of it. I don't know what I'm saying half the time.

RICH How the fuck do you think I feel? My lover leaves me; my family won't let me near them; I lose my business; I can't pay my rent. How the fuck do you think I feel?

SAUL You'll stay here with me.

RICH Till death do us part.

SAUL I love you.

RICH I don't want your love!

SAUL Take what you can . . . [get]! I didn't mean that. I love you. I always have. You have nowhere to go. You've got to stay with me.

RICH Shit shit shit.

SAUL You were kidding about picking up people.

RICH What do you think? What would you do in my place?

SAUL I wouldn't . . . I'd . . . Therapy! . . . I don't know what I'd do.
(We're back in the bar)

PICKUP 2 Jesus, I've told you all about myself. I've really spilled my guts to you. I *needed* to do that. Maybe I shouldn't say this, but, Christ, you know something? I like you very much. Even though you *are* a writer . . . Would you like to come home with me?

RICH I'd like to very much . . . *(He checks his watch)* but I have an appointment.

PICKUP 2 Then tomorrow, how about tomorrow? I don't want to lose track of you. I don't know when I've had such a good time. I can *talk* to you.

RICH I've enjoyed myself, too.

PICKUP 2 Then maybe we'll have dinner, maybe go to the movies. Do you like movies? There's an Alfred Hitchcock festival at the Regency. Or maybe we could see the new Charles Ludlam—

RICH Thanks, but I have to tell you something. I have—

PICKUP 2 You have a lover. I knew it. You're too nice to be unattached.

RICH I have . . . I have . . . I have a lover.
(We're back with SAUL*)*

SAUL You have a lover.

RICH I don't even know where he is.

SAUL I don't mean Chet. I mean me. (RICH *turns away. He's back in the bar with another stranger,* CLONE 1, *who is wearing a leather jacket and reflecting aviator glasses.* SAUL *continues to plead to* RICH*'s back)* What about me?
(RICH *tries in vain to get* CLONE 1*'s attention)*

RICH Pardon me.

SAUL What about me?

RICH Yo. Yoo-hoo. Hello.

SAUL What about *me?!*

RICH *(To* CLONE 1) What about me?!

CLONE 1 What about you?

RICH I'm a very interesting guy. You look like a very interesting guy. Let's talk. And if you don't want to talk, let's go back there and let's . . . (RICH *stares* CLONE 1 *straight in the face)* I'll do anything you want. Anything.

CLONE 1 I want you to move about three feet over to the left. Can't you see I'm cruising that dude over there? *(We notice for the first time an identically dressed man standing across the room)*

RICH Well, fuck you.

CLONE 1 What's that, buddy?
(RICH *turns his back on* CLONE 1 *and starts talking loudly to the* BARTENDER)

RICH Gimme a Jack Daniels straight up—*no* ice—make it a double, and a Heinekens chaser.

BARTENDER Double Jack up, Heinie back.
(CLONE 2 *has moseyed on over to* CLONE 1. *They stand side by side, facing the audience, feigning indifference to each other)*

CLONE 2 Your name Chip?

RICH No ice!

BARTENDER No ice.

CLONE 1 Chuck.

RICH Hate ice.

CLONE 2 *(Extending his hand)* Chad.
(The CLONES *shake hands)*

RICH *(To the* BARTENDER) Put 'er there, Chet—I mean Chump. You come here often?
(He downs the shot and beer as quickly as he can)

CLONE 2 Thought you were this guy Chip I met here on Jockstrap Night.

CLONE 1 Haven't been here since the Slave Auction.

CLONE 2 Look familiar.
(With synchronized actions the CLONES *turn to look at each other, then turn away)*

CLONE 1 Go to the Saint?

CLONE 2 Been there.

RICH *(To the* BARTENDER) Quiet for a Friday . . .

CLONE 1 I know where.

RICH Not much action.

CLONE 2 St. Mark's?

RICH *(Offering his glass)* Same . . .

CLONE 1 Nah.

RICH Probably's this disease thing.

CLONE 1 Everard. Ever go there?

CLONE 2 Stopped going since this disease thing.

CLONE 1 Gotta be real careful.

RICH Ask me, the whole thing's exaggerated. No one knows for sure how it's spread.

CLONE 2 Right. Doctor gave me a clean bill of health yesterday.

CLONE 1 Can you prove it? *(He punches* CLONE 2 *on the arm)* Kidding.

CLONE 2 Gotta be real careful. Run six miles a day.

RICH My philosophy is: you've got it, you've got it. Nothing you can do about it. *(He offers his glass)* Same.

CLONE 1 *(Tweeking* CLONE 2*'s nipple)* So what're you up for?

CLONE 2 Come right to the point, don't you?
(The CLONES *perform a macho mating ritual of arm wrestling, punching, and ass grabbing to determine who is the "top man")*

RICH Poor bastards that got it: cancer, pneumonia, herpes all over. I mean, I'd kill myself if I had to go through all that shit. Get a gun and perform fellatio on it . . .

CLONE 2 What're you up for, Daddy?

RICH Slash my wrists *with* the grain . . .

CLONE 1 Me top.

RICH Subway tracks?

CLONE 1 Got some beautiful . . .
(He snorts deeply to indicate cocaine)

CLONE 2 Ever do opium?

CLONE 1 I have a water pipe. We'll smoke it through some Southern Comfort.

RICH Or maybe I'd mix myself a Judy Garland: forty reds and a quart of vodka. *(He hands his glass to the* BARTENDER) Fuck the beer!

CLONE 1 We're roommates now. What about you?

RICH *(The ecstatic drunken poet)* "Glory be to God for dappled things . . ."

CLONE 2 I'm free, white, and twenty-four.

RICH "For skies of couple-colour as a brinded cow . . ."

SAUL I know it sounds stupid, but take care of your health.

RICH "For rose-moles all in stipple upon trout that swim . . ."

CLONE 2 In bed, I mean.

RICH I don't care what anybody says, I believe that somewhere, you know, *deep down* . . .
(He holds out his glass)

CLONE 1 I'll do anything you want.

RICH Beyond all this incredible pain and confusion, anxiety, fear, terror . . .
(He holds out his glass)

BARTENDER No ice.

CLONE 2 Anything?

RICH I believe that there might be . . . *(He searches for words to describe the Supreme Being)* that there could be . . . that there is—

CLONE 1 *Anything.*

SAUL You're drinking too much.

RICH I believe in a perfect . . .
*(*RICH *is having a booze-fueled vision of the Godhead)*

CLONE 2 Mirrors . . .

RICH Shining . . .

CLONE 1 Chains . . .

RICH Powerful . . .

SAUL Vitamins . . .

RICH Pure . . .
(A third CLONE *appears)*

CLONE 3 Rubber . . .

CLONE 1 Dildo . . .

SAUL Diet . . .

RICH Free . . .

CLONE 2 Dungeon . . .

SAUL Acupuncture . . .

RICH Truthful . . .

CLONE 3 Ten inches . . .

SAUL Interferon . . .

RICH Beautiful . . .

CLONE 3 *(Approaching the bar, to the* BARTENDER*)* Beer!

(CLONE 3 *accidentally spills beer on* RICH)

CLONE 2 Watersports.

RICH *(Raging drunkenly)* Asshole!

CLONE 1 Hey!

RICH I'll kill ya, faggot!

SAUL *(Intervening)* Hey! . . . He's been drinking.

BARTENDER Get that jerk outta here!

RICH What's a matter, can't you fight like a man?

SAUL *(Gently but firmly)* Rich.

RICH Fuck all that shit!

SAUL Rich.

RICH Let Him cure me!

SAUL *(Trying to distract him)* Did you hear the one about the faggot, the black, and the Jew?

RICH *(Shaking his fist, to God in the sky)* You hear me, motherfucker?

SAUL How did that go?

RICH Cure me!
(They are out on the street by now)

SAUL C'mon, keep moving.

RICH I'm a very bad person.

SAUL You're an asshole.

RICH I wanted to go to bed with that guy.

SAUL I practically beg you to move in—

RICH I wasn't going to tell him about me or anything.

SAUL And what do you do?

RICH But you want to know something?

SAUL You disappear for two weeks.

RICH I wouldn't do that. I would *never* do that.

SAUL I almost called the cops.

RICH You believe me?

SAUL Believe what?

RICH I never never never would ever do that.

SAUL Do you remember the one about the Polish Lesbian?

RICH Never.

SAUL She liked men.
(The joke pretty much sobers RICH *up)*

RICH You asshole.

SAUL You schmuck.

RICH You prick.

SAUL God, I miss talking dirty.

RICH Talking dirty makes it feel like spring. *(He is the superstud)* Suck my dick, faggot.

SAUL *(Superstud)* Kiss my ass, cocksucker.

RICH Sit on it, punk.

SAUL Lick boot, fruit.

RICH God, how I love sleaze: the whining self-pity of a rainy Monday night in a leather bar in early spring; five o'clock in the morning in the Mineshaft, with the bathtubs full of men dying to get pissed on and whipped; a subway john full of horny high school students; Morocco—getting raped on a tombstone in Marrakesh. God, how I miss it.

SAUL I miss my filthy old ripped-up, patched button-fly jeans that I sun-bleached on myself our first weekend on the Island. Remember? It was Labor Day—

RICH Memorial Day.

SAUL And we did blotter acid. Remember acid before they put the speed in it? And we drank muscadet when we got thirsty.

RICH Which we did a lot.

SAUL Remember?

RICH Remember Sunday afternoons blitzed on beer?

SAUL And suddenly it's Sunday night and you're getting fucked in the second-floor window of the Hotel Christopher and you're being cheered on by a mob of hundreds of men.

RICH And suddenly it's Friday a week later, and he's moved in, sleeping next to you, and you want him to go because you've met his brother Rod or Lance—

SAUL *(Practically sighing)* Miles.

RICH —late of the merchant marines, who's even humpier.

SAUL Orgies at the baths—

RICH Afternoons at the Columbus Avenue bookstore. *(They are in the back room of a gay porno shop, or "bookstore." They play their favorite bookstore habitués)*

RICH More! *Give* it to me!

SAUL Give it to *you?* Give it to *me!* Get out of my way, he's mine!

RICH No, he's mine! Keep your hands off my wallet!

SAUL *(A black queen)* Sistuhs, theyuh's plenty heah fo' ivrybody.

RICH *(A tough New York queen)* Hey, Mary, the line forms at the rear.

SAUL And whose rear might that be, sugar? *(Two other men appear in the bookstore)*

MARTY Hey, Vinnie?

VINNIE Marty?

MARTY What are you doing here? You said you were gonna buy the papers.

VINNIE You said you were gonna walk the dogs.

MARTY You trash!
(They exit, bickering)

SAUL I always knew when you were fucking around.

RICH You did your share.

SAUL *Moi?*

RICH I know why Grand Union wouldn't deliver to our house.
(They have returned to the loft)

SAUL God, I used to love promiscuous sex.

RICH Not "promiscuous," Saul, nondirective, noncommitted, nonauthoritarian—

SAUL Free, wild, rampant—

RICH Hot, sweaty, steamy, smelly—

SAUL Juicy, funky, hunky—

RICH Sex.

SAUL Sex. God, I miss it.
(RICH *lowers his eyes.* SAUL *nods and goes to* RICH. *He takes* RICH*'s face in both hands and tries to kiss him square on the mouth.* RICH *pulls away frantically)*

RICH NO!

SAUL I don't care!

RICH You don't know what you're doing!

SAUL It's my decision!

RICH *(Shaking his head)* No. Uh-uh. NO! (SAUL *sits on the sofa.* RICH *tries to take* SAUL*'s hand, but* SAUL *pulls it away. Beat)* The best times for me were going out with you on shoots.

SAUL I thought you found them boring.

RICH I enjoyed them.

SAUL I was always afraid of boring you.

RICH Remember staying up all night shooting the harvest moon at Jake's place?

SAUL My fingers got so cold I could barely change film.

RICH It was almost as bright as daylight. Remember the apple tree stuck out in the middle of the pasture, how the moonlight drained it of color?

SAUL I remember the smell of the blanket we took from the barn.

RICH Remember, I bet you I could find five constellations?

SAUL You found six . . . I never wanted us to break up.

RICH Passive aggression.

SAUL I wanted things to always remain the same. I'm still like that. I even like eating the same things day after day.

RICH Pork chops, French fries—

SAUL No change. I used to love our routine together. I'd go to work and then you'd be there when I got home, writing—

RICH Drinking.

SAUL I'd do this and you'd do that, and then we'd . . . *(He makes a graceful gesture to indicate making love)* for a while—while *Mission Impossible*'d be on low in the background.

RICH And then *Star Trek.*

SAUL I never got tired of the same—

RICH We were stagnating.

SAUL —day after day the same, so we'd have a structure to fall back on when life dealt us its wild cards or curve balls. I want to be just half awake, like at the seashore, watching the waves roll in late in the afternoon, hypnotized by the glare of the sun, smelling the sea breeze and suntan lotion. *(Beat)*

Mom is what? She's lying there next to Dad on the Navaho blanket, with white gunk on her nose, and my baby sister has finally stopped screaming and is sucking on the ear of her dollie. And Aunt Ellie—the one who said she thought I had good taste when she met you—is snoring next to husband number three. Her bazooms are going up and down, up and down, almost popping out of her bathing suit. It's so peaceful. *(Long pause)*

I was at the St. Mark's baths soaking in the hot tub when I first heard about AIDS. It was four years ago. My friend Brian—remember him?—was soaking, too, and he told me about a mutual friend who had died the week before. It was "bizarre," he said . . .

(A group enters, quietly talking)

1ST MAN The first time I heard about AIDS it was a spring day, kind of warm. I was wearing a jacket.
I remember I ran into a friend on the corner of Fifty-seventh and Broadway. He asked me if I'd heard about Joel. It didn't make any sense to me.

2ND MAN The first time I heard about AIDS was in the Paradise Garage, a disco I used to go to. I won a raffle, the proceeds of which went to help people with this strange new disease. I didn't even know what it was.

3RD MAN I thought AIDS was like Legionnaires' disease, or toxic shock syndrome, or sickle-cell anemia, Alzheimer's disease—one of those rare diseases you read about in the papers.

1ST WOMAN It seemed so terribly remote at the time, like an . . .

1ST WOMAN and 2ND MAN . . . epidemic in India . . .

1ST WOMAN and 2ND and 3RD MAN Finland . . .

1ST WOMAN and 1ST–3RD MAN Borneo . . .

1ST and 2ND WOMAN, 1ST–3RD MAN Java . . .

ALL Ethiopia

PHOTOS: © 1985 BY GERRY GOODSTEIN

HOTO:
o right: Ken Kliban, Mark Myers (behind Kliban), an Hadary, Claris Erickson, Lily Knight, Jonathan n, Lou Liberatore, Steven Gregan.

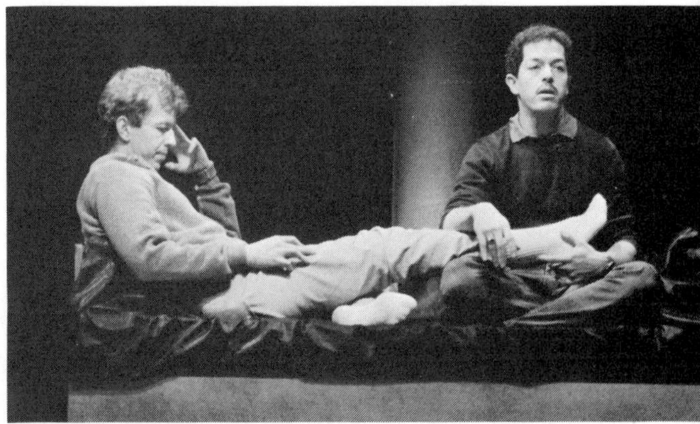

Jonathan Hogan, Jonathan Hadary

Jonathan Hadary, Lily Knight

Jonathan Hogan, Lou Liberatore

Lou Liberatore, Jonathan Hogan, Lily Knight, Mark Myers, Ken Kliban.

Ken Kliban, Lou Liberatore

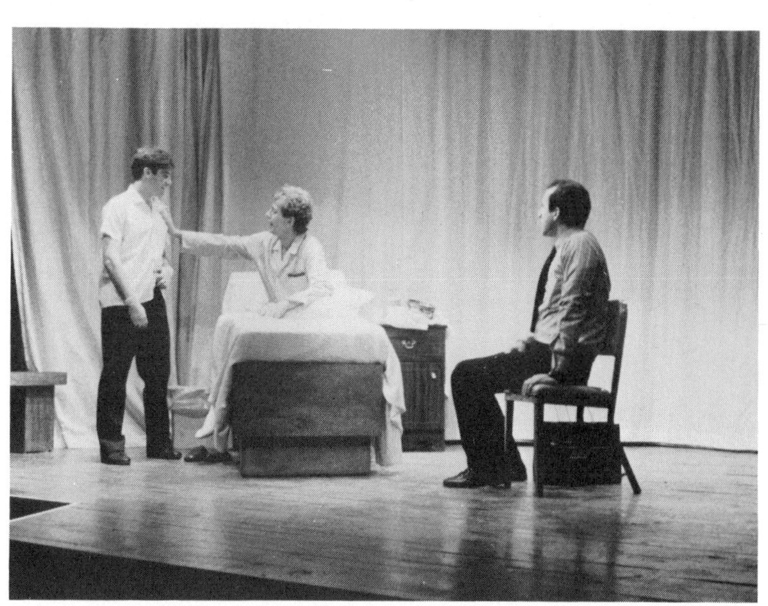

Lou Liberatore, Jonathan Hogan, Ken Kliban

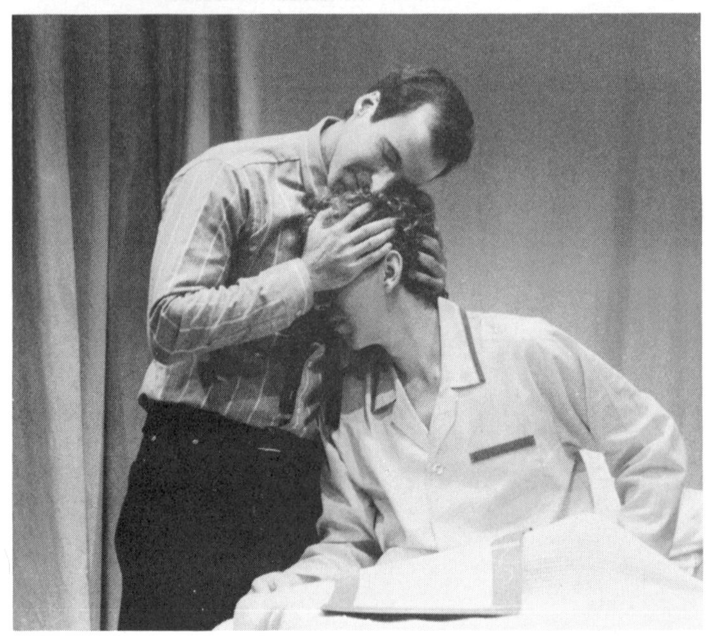

Ken Kliban, Jonathan Hogan

Claris Erickson

2ND WOMAN The first time I heard about it . . .

1ST and 2ND WOMAN . . . I was standing in my kitchen . . .

1ST WOMAN . . . I was about to go out shopping . . .

1ST and 2ND WOMAN . . . for my youngest's birthday party.

4TH MAN The phone rang.

2ND WOMAN It was this doctor calling me . . .

2ND WOMAN and 3RD MAN . . . about my son Bernard.

1ST WOMAN He used all these words I can't pronounce . . .

1ST and 2ND WOMAN . . . and then he said . . .

1ST and 4TH MAN . . . "Do you understand what I've told you?"

2ND WOMAN I said . . .

1ST and 2ND WOMAN . . . Yes.

1ST WOMAN Right before he hung up he said . . .

1ST MAN "So you know he has . . ."

ALL ". . . AIDS."

1ST WOMAN That's the first time I heard the word.

2ND WOMAN I was backstage at Saratoga.

2ND WOMAN and 4TH MAN I can't remember if it was *The Seagull* . . .

1ST WOMAN . . . or *Virginia Woolf.*

2ND WOMAN It was absurd. I had just seen him two weeks before. But there you had it . . .

3RD MAN When I first heard that Bill had AIDS and was dying, I thought . . .

2ND MAN I almost died laughing.

1ST, 2ND, 4TH MAN, 1ST and 2ND WOMAN . . . George was dead. *(The group exits)*

3RD MAN . . . my God, we're all going to die.

SAUL . . . and he told me about a mutual friend who had died the week before. It was "bizarre," he said. Brian died last week of the same thing. And he and I once soaked in the same hot tub, making a kind of human soup . . . That's all I ever wanted to do was relax. (*Long pause)* You'll stay with me. I won't bother you.

RICH Just until I feel better.

SAUL I understand: you're not coming back to be my lover.

RICH Right. Is that okay?

SAUL Schmuck. *(He mimics him)* Is that okay? Is that okay? It's *okay!* Asshole. Who the fuck wants you anyhow? And when I have guests stay the night, you disappear into your room. Right?

RICH Right. Understood. *(Offhand)* You seeing somebody?

SAUL I said when I have guests.

RICH You planning an orgy?

SAUL Just so we understand each other.

RICH I should mention one thing.

SAUL No, you do not have to spend Passover with the tribe.

RICH I miss your father.

SAUL Then go live with him. He *likes* you. The two of you could be very happy together.

RICH One thing.

SAUL He's never really liked me.

RICH Saul.

SAUL He's always been polite but—

RICH Are you finished?

SAUL No, I will not bring you coffee in bed. I only do that for lovers. Besides, I broke your blue mug.

RICH Saul, please.

SAUL On purpose.

RICH One thing. I'm embarrassed. I'm just about broke. The doctors. Tests.

SAUL I thought you were insured.

RICH They're pulling a fast one.

SAUL We'll sue. I'll call Craig. He'll know what—

RICH Craig told me not to have high hopes.

SAUL We'll get by. You'll see.

RICH I'll keep track of every cent you spend on me. You'll get it all back when I can work. I swear.

SAUL Not to worry, I'll take it out in trade.

RICH Saul, I'm frightened!

(SAUL *takes him in his arms)*

SAUL We'll be okay, we'll be okay . . .

(They hold each other. LILY *walks into the scene with* CHET. *She's dressed in evening wear and is carrying a number of accessories, including a mirror and a shawl.* CHET *is dressed in cutoffs and a sweatshirt. We are in a flashback)*

LILY Rich, congratulations! It's fantastic that they're going to publish your book.

(SAUL *tries to break from the clinch, but* RICH *holds him back)*

RICH No autographs, please.

LILY It's wonderful, it really is, but can you guys celebrate later?

SAUL *(To* RICH) Let me go. *(To* CHET) How do you do? I'm Saul.

LILY Shit. Saul, Rich—my cousin Chet.

SAUL *(Trying to shake hands)* Hi, Chet. *(To* RICH) You're strangling me.

CHET Hi.

RICH *(To* SAUL) It's your last chance to kiss the author before he becomes famous and goes straight.

SAUL Straight to the baths. *(To* CHET) So how do you like New York?

CHET I only got here yesterday. Lily's taking me to a show tonight.

RICH Do you think success will change me?

SAUL God, I hope so.

LILY I know I'm being a pig, but I need head shots by six o'clock. *(She lowers a roller of colored background paper)* It's a dazzling role for me and *(To* SAUL) you're such an artist.

SAUL Rich is the "artiste" in the family.

LILY Chet, be an angel and bring Saul his camera. It's by the bar.

(CHET *looks for the camera)*

SAUL *(To* CHET) Don't let your cousin push you around the way she does me.

LILY Come on, Saul, make click-click.

SAUL Unless you like that sort of thing.

RICH That's all I get?

LILY *(To* RICH, *about* SAUL) Leave the boy alone.

RICH A hug and a bitchy remark?

SAUL *(To* RICH) That and ninety cents.

RICH *(To* SAUL) No "Gee, Rich, I'm so proud of you"?

SAUL *(Smiling falsely)* Gee, Rich, I'm so proud of you.

RICH I finally have some good news and he's annoyed.

CHET *(Holding the camera, to* LILY) What should I do with this?

SAUL Well, your brother called, while you were out guzzling lunch with your agent, Dr. Mengele. Call him back.

RICH What'd he have to say?

SAUL Call him and ask him. I'm not your secretary.

RICH *(Imitating him)* I'm not your—

SAUL He forgot my fucking name again. How long we been together?

RICH Too long. Forget my brother. It's my first fucking book. Let's celebrate.

SAUL You celebrate.

LILY I'll throw a party.

RICH What'll you serve, organic cabbage juice?

SAUL *(To* LILY) His brother's a scumbag.

RICH He likes you, too.

CHET *(Still holding the camera, to* SAUL) Do you want this?

SAUL *(To* CHET) Thanks, Chuck.

CHET Chet.

(SAUL *accepts the camera from* CHET *but ignores the correction)*

LILY *(Fondly, to* RICH) You're such a lush.

RICH Whatever happened to my old drinking buddy?

LILY Did you know they have gay A.A. meetings?

(RICH *makes a face)*

SAUL *(To* RICH, *trying to be nice)* It's great news, babes, really.

RICH You really don't give a fuck.

SAUL Just how many copies you think a book of "fairy tales" will sell?

LILY I picked a fine day to have my picture taken.

SAUL If you only knew how much I love doing head shots.

RICH *(To* SAUL) Ah, fuck it, I guess I'm being childish.

SAUL I shouldn't have said that. I'm thoughtless.

(RICH *shrugs)*

LILY And I'm Sneezy. No, really, I'm selfish. But I want that role so bad. I play the ghost of Marie Antoinette. *(Throwing the scarf around her neck and taking a tits-and-ass pose, she speaks to* SAUL) How do you like this, hon? "Let them eat . . ."

(She drops the pose immediately as SAUL *starts to photograph her)*

SAUL Move your head a little to the . . . *(She moves her head)* Good.

(SAUL *snaps her)*

RICH *(Going to living area, followed by* CHET) I'm going running.

(RICH *changes into jogging clothes)*

CHET How far do you run?

RICH Depends. I'm in training for the marathon.

CHET The marathon! Hey, that's great. I run, too.

RICH Oh, yeah?

(LILY *and* SAUL *are busy taking pictures in the other side of the loft. They can see* RICH *and* CHET, *but they can't easily hear them)*

LILY How's this?

CHET Congratulations on the book.

RICH Thanks.

SAUL That's right.

LILY I forget the director's name. He's Lithuanian.

CHET That poem of yours that Lily has hung up in her kitchen, I read it. I think it's great.

SAUL Great.

RICH You don't much look like the poetry type.

LILY Bulgarian.

CHET I'm not. I just love your poem.

RICH Are you a student?

CHET Just graduated from San Francisco State.

LILY Everybody in the play is dead.

SAUL Your cousin's hot. Is he gay?

LILY I don't know. I'll ask him. *(She yells to* CHET) Chet, are you gay?

SAUL Christ.

RICH That's what I call tact.

LILY Well?

CHET *(Loud, to* LILY) Yes.

LILY Thanks, hon.

SAUL Give us a little more cheek . . .

CHET There's a line of your poem I don't understand.

RICH Only one? I have no idea what any of it means.

CHET "The final waning moon . . ."

SAUL Don't smile.

RICH "And the coming of the light."

CHET I love the way it sounds.

SAUL Smile.

CHET "The final waning moon / And the coming of the light."

SAUL *(Indicating to Lily that he wants a sexy pose)* He loves you.

CHET Oh, I get it.

RICH Lily tells me you're looking for a place to stay.

CHET New York is so expensive.

SAUL He lusts for you.

RICH A friend of mine wants someone to take care of his loft while he's in L.A.

SAUL He wants to ravage you.

CHET I'll do it.

RICH He has eight cats.

CHET Eight tigers, I don't care.

LILY I love that play.

RICH It's in Tribeca.

SAUL *(Yelling to* RICH) I apologize about the book.
(RICH *and* CHET *ignore* SAUL)

CHET Where's Tribeca?

SAUL Did you hear me?

RICH On the isle of Manhattan.

CHET We're on the isle of Manhattan.

RICH We are.

LILY The main characters are all ghosts.

CHET I know that.

SAUL I'll throw him a party.

RICH That's about all you have to know.

SAUL A big bash.

CHET Is it?

LILY He'll love that.

RICH I'll tell you a few more things.

CHET Will you?

SAUL I'll even invite his brother.

RICH You bet your ass I will.

SAUL *(Snapping up the roller of background paper)* Finished.

*(*LILY, RICH, *and* CHET *leave.* SAUL *goes to the sofa. The* HOSPICE WORKER *comes forward)*

HOSPICE WORKER A woman is told by her doctor that she has cancer and has only a month to live. "Now wait just one minute," she tells the doctor. "I'll be wanting a second opinion." To which the doctor replies, "Okay, you're ugly, too."

David told me that one. He was an old Jewish man who had survived the Lodz ghetto in World War II. He'd seen everything in his life, and when the time came for him to go, he accepted it. The doctors wanted to go to obscene lengths to keep his body alive, but he refused. I loved him.

But most of my people are more like Margaret. She was in her nineties. She half accepted the fact that she was dying. One moment she'd be talking to you about which nephew she was definitely going to cross out of her will, and the next she'd be telling you about the summer vacation she was planning in Skibbereen. She had terminal cancer! But I always go along with what they have to say. My job is not to bring enlightenment, only comfort.

Which reminds me: Margaret's family saw her as some kind of prophet. The whole clan was in the room waiting to hear her last words. She had developed a distinct dislike for her family, so I was sitting closest to her when she went, and therefore I could hear what the poor soul was whispering. After it was all over, they asked me what prayer she had been uttering. I told them the Lord's Prayer. I didn't have the heart to tell them that what she was saying was "Oh, shit, oh, shit, oh, shit."

I've worked with thirty-five people altogether. About a third of them had AIDS. It *is* the Village.

(She exits. Lights come up on stage left area. An AIDS support group is in session)

PERSON WITH AIDS 1 *(A serious young man)* Funny thing is, I wasn't at all promiscuous.

PWA 4 Oh, please.

PWA 1 I swear. And I never drank much—once in a while a beer with Mexican food—and I don't smoke, and drugs, forget . . . I met Jerry in my sophomore year—we shared the same dorm room at Hofstra—and we fell in love, and that was it for me. When the sex revolution thing happened, I remember I felt retarded. Everybody was doing all those wild things. Me, I was going to the opera a lot. As far as I know, Jerry didn't screw around. He swore he didn't. But then . . . he's not around for me to cross-examine. He left me.

RICH Well, I . . .

PWA 3 What?

RICH No.

PWA 2 *(A young housewife, eight months pregnant)* At least when I come here I don't have to lie. Like "Bernie's doing better. I'm fine." I can even crack up if I want to. Don't worry, I won't do it two weeks in a row. I mean, who's there to talk to in Brewster? These things don't happen in Brewster. Police officers don't shoot up heroin, cops don't come down with the "gay plague"—that's what they call it in Brewster. I can't talk to Bernie. I'll never forgive him. Have a chat with the minister? "Well, Reverend Miller, I have this little problem. My husband has AIDS, and I have AIDS, and I'm eight months pregnant, and I . . ." You guys know what I mean. You're the only people in this world who know what I mean.

PWA 4 I was part of a team trying to teach robots how to use language. *(He moves and talks like a robot)* "I'm Harris, your android model 3135X. I can vacuum the floors, cook cheeseburgers, play the piano."

It's much harder to teach robots to understand. *(He instructs a backward robot)* "Joke." *(The robot responds dutifully)* "Noun: a clash of values or levels of reality, producing laughter. Example: 'Have you heard about the disease attacking Jewish American princesses? It's called MAIDS. You die if you *don't* get it. Ha. Ha.' "

My co-workers asked me to leave. They were afraid of contracting AIDS through the air, or by my looking at them. You see, they are scientists. My last act before I left was programming one final robot. *(He behaves like a robot again)* "Good morning. This is Jack— *(He suddenly becomes a flamboyantly gay robot)* but you can call me Jackie—your *fabulous* new android model 1069. If you wish to use me—and I love being used—press one of those cunning little buttons on my pecs. Go on, press one— *(He switches from a campy tone to an almost angry, accusatory one)* or are you afraid of me, too?"

That was my stab at immortality.

RICH I'm not sure I have it anymore. I feel guilty saying this, like somehow I'm being disloyal to the group. I'm getting better, I know it. I just have these lumps, which for some reason won't go away, and a loss of weight, which has made me lighter than I've been for years. Have you seen that commercial on TV? "Lose ten, twenty, thirty pounds! Lose weight the AYDS way."

PWA 3 They're going to have to change the name of their product.

RICH But anyway, I feel great. I feel the disease disappearing in me. Only a tiny percentage of those with the swollen glands come down with the rest. I'm going to *not* come here next week. I'm sorry.

SAUL *(Calling to* RICH *as if he were in the next room, while feeling the glands in his neck and armpits)* Rich?

RICH *(Still to group)* Why do I keep on apologizing?

SAUL Rich?

RICH If I *really* thought that I was coming down with it . . . We all have *options.*

SAUL Rich.

RICH *(Entering* SAUL*'s area)* What?

SAUL Here, feel my glands.

RICH You are such a hypochondriac.

SAUL Do you think they're swollen?

RICH *(Placing his hands around* SAUL*'s neck)* They feel okay to me. *(He continues in a Transylvanian accent)* But your neck—eet is grotesquely meesshapen. *(Suddenly he is mock-strangling* SAUL) Here, let me feex it. *(They start wrestling on sofa)*

SAUL Not fair!

RICH You're such a hypochondriac.

SAUL Ow! *I'm* such a hypochondriac. You and your vitamins!

RICH You and your yoga!

SAUL You and your yogurt!

RICH It's working. My ratio's up.

SAUL All right! *(He sings, to the tune of "New York, New York")*

T-cells up,
The suppressors are down.
New York, New York . . .

RICH Hey, I love you! You know that?

SAUL If you love me, get off my chest!

RICH I don't dare. You'd try and get even. You're that way.

SAUL We'll call a truce. One, two, three . . .

RICH and SAUL Truce.

(As RICH *climbs off* SAUL*'s chest,* SAUL *pulls him down, lifting his shirt, and gets him in a hammerlock)*

SAUL You were right. You never should have trusted me.

RICH Unfair . . . foul . . . most unfair!

SAUL Fuck fair. The winner gets his way with the loser. *(They tussle until* RICH *gives up)* Having vanquished the good ship *Socrates,* the savage pirate chief Bigmeat takes the first mate as his captive.

RICH *(In falsetto)* No, Captain Bigmeat, no!

SAUL I've had me eye on ye since that time we met in Bangalore. Ye can't escape me now, matey. I shall ravish ye fer sure.

(SAUL *tickles* RICH)

RICH No! . . . I'm pure of blood and noble born! *(Gradually their play turns more and more sexual, which* RICH *resists at first)* No! . . . No! . . . *(He relents)* Perhaps . . . Please!

SAUL Now I got ye, boy-o . . . boy-o . . . boy-o . . . Oh, boy!

(Finally RICH *stops struggling.* RICH *and* SAUL *are close together, panting, exhausted.* SAUL *is about to make love to* RICH *when he notices a mark on his back)*

RICH What?

(SAUL *ignores him and looks at the mark carefully)*

RICH What? You seduce me, you finally succeed in getting me hot and bothered, and what do you do as I lie here panting? You look at my birthmark.

SAUL Not the birthmark.
(He looks at RICH*'s back. He touches some marks)*

RICH What is it?

SAUL Nothing.

RICH What is it? Tell me!

SAUL I'm sure it's nothing!

RICH What! WHAT! *WHAT!* . . .
(Immediately, the HOSPICE WORKER *draws a curtain that surrounds the entire living area of* SAUL*'s loft, hiding it from view. Overlapping the closing of the curtain, we hear the ringing of two telephones. The lights come up on two men sitting side by side, answering multiline telephones)*

PAT Hotline, Pat speaking.

BARNEY Hotline. This is Barney. *(Covering the phone, he speaks to* PAT*)* Oh, no, it's her again.

PAT Are you a gay man?

BARNEY Didn't we speak a few days ago? *(Covering the phone, to* PAT*)* She doesn't stop.

PAT We're all worried.

BARNEY Is he bisexual?

PAT Calm down, first of all.
(The third line rings)

BARNEY Is he an IV drug user?

PAT It's not all that easy to get it—*if* you take a few precautions. *(Covering the phone, to* BARNEY) Okay, I'll get it. *(He speaks into the phone)* Please hold on.
(He presses a button)

BARNEY It wasn't my intention to insult you.

PAT Hotline . . . Shit. *(Pressing a button, he speaks to* BARNEY) Lost him. Fucking phone.

BARNEY So what makes you think he has AIDS?

PAT *(To phone)* Hello.

BARNEY He is what?

PAT The disease is spread mainly through the blood and the semen.

BARNEY American Indians are *not* a risk group. *(He covers the phone and speaks to* PAT) American Indians?

PAT So wear a rubber.

BARNEY There's half a zillion diseases he has symptoms of.

PAT Make *him* wear a rubber.
(The phone rings)

BARNEY Please hold.
(He presses a button)

PAT Kissing is questionable.

BARNEY Hotline . . . *(He's responding to a hate call)* And your mother eats turds in hell! . . . Thank you.
(He presses a button)

PAT Myself, I don't do it on the first date.

BARNEY I would definitely check it out with a physician.

BARNEY Spots? I'm not a doctor . . . Go to a doctor.

PAT Stroking, holding, rubbing, mirrors, whips, chains, jacking off, porno—use your imagination.

BARNEY I'm sorry you're lonely.

PAT Just don't exchange any body fluids and you'll be all right.

BARNEY Madam, we're busy here. I can't stay on the line with you all day.

PAT You have a nice voice, too, but I'm seeing someone.

BARNEY Hello?

PAT Thanks.

BARNEY *(To* PAT*)* Thank God.

PAT Good luck.
(They hang up at the same time)

BARNEY Spots. I love it.

PAT *(To himself)* I am not seeing anyone.

BARNEY What are you talking about?

PAT I was saying how much I love being celibate. *(He kisses his palm)* So how the fuck are you?

BARNEY Tired, broke, depressed, and Tim is moving out this afternoon. Well, you asked. I hear you have a new PWA.*

PAT Sorry about Tim. Yes, I have a new baby. Why do I get all the tough customers?

BARNEY Because you're so tough.

PAT So butch.

BARNEY So mean.

PAT Weathered by life like the saddle under a cowboy's ass.

BARNEY Ooooh. I could never be a CIW.† Where do you get your energy?

PAT Drugs. I don't do that anymore either. What *do* I do? I wait tables, answer phones, and work with ingrates like Rich. Boy, is he pissed. He calls me Miss Nightingale or Florence and throws dishes and curses his roommate and won't cooperate with the doctor and won't see his shrink and isn't interested in support groups *and he shit in the fucking bathtub!* He shit—

BARNEY Is he incontinent?

PAT Fuck, no. He ain't that sick yet. He said it was "convenient." I don't know why he shit in the tub.

BARNEY A real sweetheart.

PAT I'm going out of my mind. Thank God they put him in the hospital.

* Person With AIDS.

† Crisis Intervention Worker.

BARNEY First time?

PAT Yep.

BARNEY I'd probably be a real bastard.

PAT I wouldn't take it lying down.

BARNEY You'd take it any way you can get it.

PAT Go on, girl friend.

BARNEY Me, if I learned I had it, I'd shove a time bomb up my tush and drop in on Timmy for tea and meet his new lover: Jimmy.

PAT Jimmy?

BARNEY I swear: Jimmy. *(He is visiting Timmy and Jimmy for high tea)* "Timmy has told me so much about you. I've been *dying* to meet you." And kaboom! there goes Timmy and Jimmy.

PAT Timmy and Jimmy?
(The telephone rings)

BARNEY Ain't it a gas?

PAT Gag me, for sure.

BARNEY For sure.

PAT *(Answering the phone)* Hotline. Pat speaking.

BARNEY *(Raging)* When are we going to get some more help around here??!! I'm going out of my mind! *(Suddenly, he is sweet and sultry as he answers the phone)* Hotline, Barney speaking.

PAT Are you a gay man?

BARNEY Are you a gay man?
(The lights quickly fade on the two men. The curtain opens, revealing a hospital room, with bed, chair, and bed table. The loft space and bar have disappeared. RICH *is in bed.* LILY, SAUL, *and a nurse are standing nearby.)*

NURSE Temperature and blood pressure, Mr. Farrell.

LILY Can you come back later?

SAUL He's had some bad news.

NURSE He's last on my rounds.

RICH *(To* SAUL) You lied to me.

SAUL I didn't know.

LILY He didn't know. I swear.

NURSE It'll just take a minute.

RICH What other little details are you keeping from me? They let him lie there like a dog. What else? *(A Hispanic hospital worker comes in to empty the waste basket)* You! *Váyase!* Get the wetback out of here! *Váyase!*

HOSPITAL WORKER I not do nothing! He crazy.

RICH You, get out of here before I breathe on you! *Ahora! Ahora! Váyase!*

NURSE Mr. Farrell, please.

SAUL Come back later. *Más tarde, por favor.*

RICH Go back to your picket line. *(To* SAUL*)* They want a wage hike, no less. He tried to get me to bribe him to clean my room—

HOSPITAL WORKER *Qué coño estás diciendo?* [What the fuck are you saying?]

NURSE Please cooperate.

LILY He didn't say anything.

RICH He won't go near my bed, but he's not afraid to touch my money.

SAUL You misunderstood him.

RICH *El dinero está limpio, ah? Tu madre.* [Money is clean, huh, motherfucker?]

HOSPITAL WORKER *Maricón.* [Faggot.]

RICH *(To* SAUL*)* They're unionizing primates now.

LILY *(To* RICH*)* Sh!

HOSPITAL WORKER *No entiendo.* [I don't understand.] I going.

(The HOSPITAL WORKER *exits)*

LILY *(Aside to* SAUL*)* I shouldn't have told him about Chet.

SAUL *(Aside to* LILY*)* Better you than someone else.

RICH *(Imitating* LILY *and* SAUL*)* Bzzz bzzz bzzz.

NURSE *(Trying to put a blood-pressure cuff on* RICH*'s arm)* Will you be still a moment so I can check your blood pressure?

RICH Are you a union member, too?

NURSE *(To* SAUL) What shall I do?

LILY A good friend of his just passed away.

NURSE AIDS?
(She resumes struggling with the cuff)

RICH The undertakers' union. Go away, I'm on strike, too; I refuse to participate in the documentation of my own demise.

SAUL She's only trying to help you.

RICH *(Ripping off the cuff, to the* NURSE) Go find another statistic for the Center for Disease Control.

NURSE *(To* SAUL) I'm a patient woman, but he wants me to lose it. I swear that's what he's after.

RICH Lady, fuck off!

SAUL *(To the* NURSE) Please. Can't you see he's upset?

NURSE *(To* RICH) Okay, you win. I'm losing it. Are you happy? I'm *angry,* angry, Mr. Farrell.

LILY Will you please go!

NURSE A person can take only so much. I give up. I don't have to put up with this shit. I'm gonna speak to my supervisor.
(The NURSE *leaves)*

RICH *(Applauding)* Three gold stars for self-assertion!

LILY *(To* SAUL) I should have kept my mouth shut.

RICH Having brought Romeo the news that Juliet is dead, Balthasar makes a tearful exit.

LILY I don't know what to say.
(LILY *looks at* RICH, *then* SAUL)

RICH I said: Balthasar makes a tearful exit.

LILY I know how you're feeling.

RICH No matter. Get thee gone and hire those horses.

LILY I loved Chet, too.

RICH Tush, thou art deceived.

LILY He told me he was sorry for the way he treated you.

RICH Do the thing I bid thee.

LILY He didn't belong in New York. He thought he was so sophisticated, but he was just a kid from Mendocino. I'm sorry I let him go home.

RICH The messenger must go. The hero wishes to be alone with his confidant.
(RICH *turns his back on* SAUL *and* LILY)

LILY I'll be back tomorrow. *(Aside to* SAUL) I've got half a crown roast from Margo. She went vegetarian. I'll be up. I'm arranging a memorial service for Chet at St. Joe's. (SAUL *indicates that* LILY *should leave. She gathers up her belongings, mimes dialing a telephone, and blows* SAUL *a kiss)* Rich?
(SAUL *shakes his head no. She leaves.* SAUL *tries to think of something to say to* RICH. *He abandons the effort and picks up the Sunday* New York Times *crossword puzzle)*

SAUL "African quadruped." *(He writes) G-n-u . . .* "Hitler's father." *(He counts on his fingers)* One, two . . . five letters. Let's see: Herman? Herman Hitler? *(He counts)* That's six . . . Otto? . . . Werner? . . . Rudi? . . . Putzi? *(He shrugs)* Fuck. *(He reads on)* Thank God: "Jewish rolls." Starts with a *b,* six letters: bagels. *(He starts to write it in)* Shit, that won't work. I need a *y.*

RICH *(Without turning)* Bialys.

SAUL *B-i-a-l-y-s.*

RICH Short for Bialystok, a large industrial city in eastern Poland . . . *(He turns to* SAUL) hometown of Ludwig Zamenhof, inventor of Esperanto, an artificial international language. Alois Hitler: *A-l-o—*

SAUL *(Putting down puzzle)* Outclassed again. Why do I bother? He knows everything.

RICH When I was a kid I used to spend all my time in libraries. My childhood was—

SAUL If I had a father like yours I would have done the same thing.

RICH But thanks to that son of a bitch I could tell you how many metric tons of coal the Benelux countries produced per annum, and the capital city of the Grand Duchy of Liechtenstein.

SAUL I give up.

RICH Vaduz.

SAUL Miss Trivial Pursuit.

RICH I knew to which great linguistic family the Telegu language of South India belongs.

SAUL Telegu? Isn't that the national dish of Botswana?

RICH *(Ignoring him)* The Dravidian. (SAUL *straightens up the bed table)* I've always loved words . . . I wrote poetry when I was a kid. My brother used to make fun of me . . .

Winter, winter,
How you glinter,
With holidays' array.
And the snow
We all know
Is here all day.

(SAUL *smiles)*

I was eight, nine when I wrote that. I had just come in from sledding down Indian Hill, a steep road that connects Jefferson Heights to the valley.

SAUL You showed it to me on our grand tour of West Jersey.

RICH It was a late afternoon just before sundown and the sky was intensely blue and intensely cold and you could see the stars already. For some reason nobody was home when I came back, so I stood there at the stamped enamel-top kitchen table dripping in my frozen corduroys and wrote that poem.

SAUL Are you comfortable?
(RICH *shrugs.* SAUL *fixes his pillows)*

RICH I was a good kid, but I was lonely and scared all the time. I was so desperate to find people like myself that I looked for them in the indexes of books—under *h.* I eventually found them—

SAUL But not in books.

RICH The next thing you know I moved to the city and was your typical office-worker-slash-writer. I hated my job, so I grew a beard and wore sandals, hoping they would fire me and give me permanent unemployment. I wanted to stay at home in my rent-controlled apartment and drink bourbon and write poems. I did that for a period. I loved it. The apartment got filthy and I did, too, and I'd go out only at night—to pick up guys. And then I found you—in a porno theater— *(He takes* SAUL*'s hand)* and we semi-settled down and you took my picture and I started to jog. We bought a loft—

SAUL And raised a cat—

RICH —and loved each other. But that wasn't enough for me. I don't think you ever understood this: you weren't my muse, you were . . . *(He searches for the word)* Saul. (SAUL *rises and looks out the window)* I loved you but I wanted someone to write poems to. During our marriage I had almost stopped writing, and felt stifled even though our loft had appeared in *New York* magazine.

And then I met Chet and left you in the lurch and lived with him at the Chelsea Hotel. He was shallow, callow, and selfish, and I loved him, too.

We did a lot of coke and I wrote a lot of poetry and the catering was booming and *The New Yorker* published a story of mine and I ran in the marathon. I was on a roll. *(He speaks with mounting excitement as he relives the experience)* I remember training on the East River Drive for the first time. I didn't realize how narrow and dark the city streets were until I got to the river and all of a sudden there was the fucking river. The sky was the same color as that twilight when I was a kid. I came from the darkness into the light. I'm running downtown and I make this bend and out of nowhere straight up ahead is the Manhattan Bridge and then the Brooklyn Bridge, one after another, and my earphones are playing Handel's *Royal Fireworks Music.* It can't get better than this, I know it. I'm running and crying from gratitude. I came from the darkness into the light. I'm running and telling God I didn't know He was *that* good or *that* big, thank you, Jesus, thanks, thanks . . . *(He slumps back, exhausted from the effort)*

The next morning I woke up with the flu and stayed in bed for a couple of days and felt much better. But my throat stayed a little sore and my glands were a little swollen . . . *(There is a long silence.* RICH *speaks casually)* Saul, I want you to do something for me. Will you do something for me, baby?

SAUL Sure, babe.

RICH Now listen. I want you to go out of here and go to the doctor and tell him you aren't sleeping so hot—

SAUL I'm sleeping okay.

RICH Sh! Now listen: you tell him you want something to make you sleep and Valium doesn't work on you, but a friend once gave you some Seconal—

SAUL *No!* I won't do it!

RICH *(Pressuring* SAUL *relentlessly)* I tried hoarding the pills here, but every night the nurse stays to watch me swallow them down.

SAUL I can't do that.

RICH I don't want to end up like Chet.

SAUL I won't listen.

RICH If you love me, you'll help me. I have something that's eating me up. I don't want to go on. I'm scared to go on.

SAUL Don't do this to me! I can't handle it. I'll go out the window, I swear, don't do this—

RICH Don't you see, it's the only way. Just get the pills.

SAUL No!

RICH Just have them around. You'll get used to the idea. And when the lesions spread above my neck so that I don't look the same, you'll want me to have them.

SAUL Help me, help me!

RICH It's all right. Not now.

SAUL No.

RICH Tomorrow.

SAUL No.

RICH The day after.

SAUL No.

RICH We'll see.
(RICH*'s* BROTHER, *wearing a surgical mask, gown, and gloves and carrying a small shopping bag, tiptoes in, stopping when he notices* RICH *and* SAUL)

SAUL Oh, my God. I think it's your brother.

BROTHER I'll come back later.

SAUL *(Pulling himself together)* No, I was just going.

BROTHER It's all right, really.

SAUL I've been here for a while.

BROTHER I'm interrupting.

SAUL Really.

RICH *(To his* BROTHER) Unless you're planning to come into intimate contact with me or my body fluids, none of that shit you have on is necessary.

BROTHER The sign says—

RICH But please restrain your brotherly affection for my sake: who knows what diseases you might have brought in with you?

(The BROTHER *removes the mask, gown, and gloves)*

SAUL You two haven't seen each other for a while, so why don't I just—

RICH By all means. You need a break, kid. Think about what I said.

SAUL It stopped raining. I'll take a walk.

RICH Have a nice walk.

BROTHER Good seeing ya . . . ?

(He has forgotten SAUL*'s name)*

SAUL Saul. Yeah.

(SAUL *exits. Beat)*

BROTHER I owe you an apology . . . (RICH *won't help him)* I was very frightened . . . I'm afraid I panicked . . . Please forgive me.

RICH Nothing to forgive.

BROTHER *(Brightly)* Betty sends her love. She sent along a tin of butter crunch. *(He offers* RICH *a tin, which*

RICH *ignores)* You're not on any special diet? I told Betty I thought maybe you'd be on one of those macrobiotic diets. I read in the papers that it's helped some people with . . .

RICH AIDS.

BROTHER Yes. I keep a file of clippings on all the latest medical developments. *(He takes a clipping out of his wallet)* Looks like they're going to have a vaccine soon. I read that the French—

RICH That's to *prevent* AIDS. I already *have* AIDS.

BROTHER Right . . . So how are you doing?

RICH *(Smiling cheerfully)* I have Kaposi's sarcoma, a hitherto rare form of skin cancer. It's spreading. I have just begun chemotherapy. It nauseates me. I expect my hair will fall out. I also have a fungal infection of the throat called candidiasis, or thrush. My life expectancy is . . . I have a greater chance of winning the lottery. Otherwise I'm fine. How are you?

BROTHER I'm sorry . . . *(After a long pause, he speaks brightly again)* Mary Pat sends her love. She won her school swimming competition and I registered her for the South Jersey championship. Oh, I forgot, she made this for you . . .

(He takes a large handmade fold-out card from the shopping bag. It opens downward a full two feet)

RICH Say, have you heard about the miracle of AIDS?

BROTHER What?

RICH It can turn a fruit into a vegetable. What's the worst thing about getting AIDS?

(The BROTHER *lets the card fall to the floor)*

BROTHER Stop it!

RICH Trying to convince your parents that you're Haitian. Get it?

BROTHER I came here to see if I can help you.

RICH Skip it. So what do you want?

BROTHER I don't want anything.

RICH Everything I own is going to Saul—

BROTHER I don't want anything.

RICH Except for the stuff Mom left us. I told Saul that it's to go to you. Except for the Barcelona chair—

BROTHER I don't care about—

RICH I'm leaving Saul the copyright to my book—

BROTHER Why are you doing this to me?

RICH So you don't want my worldly possessions, such as they are; you want me to relieve your guilt.

BROTHER Stop it.

RICH *(Making the sign of the cross over his* BROTHER, *chanting)* I hereby exonerate you of the sin of being ashamed of your queer brother and being a coward in the face of—

BROTHER Stop! Don't!
(The BROTHER *grabs* RICH*'s hand)*

RICH No!

BROTHER Richard, don't! . . . *(He attempts to hug* RICH, *who resists with all his strength)* I don't care . . . I don't care! . . . Rich! . . . Richie . . . Richie . . .
(RICH *relents. They hug)*

RICH I'm so . . . [frightened]

BROTHER Forgive me. Forgive me.

RICH I don't want to . . . [die]

BROTHER It's all right . . . I'm here . . .
(They hold each other close for a beat. The HOSPITAL WORKER *rushes into the room)*

HOSPITAL WORKER Psst. *Oye.* Psst.
(RICH *and his* BROTHER *notice the* WORKER)

RICH What do you want now?

HOSPITAL WORKER *(Shakes his head no)* *Viene. Viene.* He come. He come.
(He pulls the BROTHER *from* RICH)

RICH Who come?

HOSPITAL WORKER *Su amigo.* Your freng. He no like.

BROTHER What's he saying?
(RICH *starts to laugh. Enter* SAUL. *The* WORKER *starts sweeping and whistling with an air of exuberant nonchalance. The following is overlapping)*

RICH *(Laughing)* He . . . he . . .

SAUL What's going on?

BROTHER Richie, what's so damned funny?

RICH He thought we . . . *(He breaks up)* that he and I were cheating on you.

BROTHER He thought that you and I were . . . *(He laughs)*

RICH He came in to warn me that you were coming! *(He laughs. To the* WORKER) *Gracias! Muchas gracias!*

SAUL He thought that you two were . . . *(He laughs)*

HOSPITAL WORKER *(To* RICH) *De nada.* [You're welcome.] Why you laugh? *(The* WORKER *laughs) Como hay maricones.* [What a bunch of faggots.]

RICH *Es mi hermano. Perdona por lo que dije antes. Yo (He points to himself) era mucho estúpido.* [He's my brother. Forgive me for what I said to you before. I was being very stupid.]

HOSPITAL WORKER *De nada. Somos todos estúpidos, chico.* [We're all stupid, my friend.]
(He leaves. The giggles subside)

BROTHER *(Checking watch, stiffening his spine)* I've got to be going now.

RICH I'm glad you came by.

BROTHER I'll be back tomorrow with Mary Pat. She's been dying—wanting to come by. She's been writing poetry and—

RICH I'd love to see her. And tell Betty thanks for the . . . ?

BROTHER Butter crunch. *(He shakes hands with* SAUL) Good seeing ya . . . ? *(He has forgotten* SAUL*'s name again)*

SAUL Saul.

BROTHER Sorry. Bye.
(He leaves)

SAUL I won't get upset. I won't get upset.

RICH What's the matter?

SAUL It's *my* problem.

RICH What?

SAUL Rich, I've thought about things.

RICH What?

SAUL *(Suddenly exploding)* Goddamn it! That prick doesn't know my name after—how many years are we together?

RICH *Were* together.

SAUL Pardon me, I forgot we got an annulment from the pope. Fuck it, I won't get upset.

RICH *(Overlapping)* My brother finds it hard to deal with the fact that—

SAUL I said fuck it.

RICH Don't you see, it was a big step for him—

SAUL Your brother hates my fucking guts. Haven't you ever told him I didn't turn you queer?

RICH My brother—

SAUL I didn't give you AIDS either.

RICH My brother—

SAUL Why're you always defending him? What about me?

RICH My brother's got a few feelings, too, even if he isn't a card-carrying member of the lavender elite.

SAUL Let's hear it from our working-class hero.

RICH You've never tried talking to him. You're so self-centered that it never occurred to you—

SAUL I'm self— Now wait one minute! I'm so self-centered that I was willing to buy the pills for you.

RICH You have the pills?
(The other actors create the sleazy atmosphere of Christopher Street near the Hudson River)

DEALER 1 Yo, my man.

SAUL I was willing to go down to Christopher Street, where all the drug dealers hang out.

DEALER 2 What's 'attenin', what's 'attenin'?
(SAUL *turns his back to* RICH *and immediately he is on Christopher Street)*

SAUL *(To* DEALER 2) Nice night.

RICH I told you to go to the doctor's.

DEALER 1 Smoke 'n' acid, MDA 'n' speed. Smoke 'n' acid, MDA 'n' speed . . .

DEALER 2 Smoke 'n' coke, smoke 'n' coke . . .

SAUL *(To* DEALER 1) I said "Nice night."

DEALER 1 Real nice. What's shakin', babe?

RICH All you would've had to say to the doctor was "My roommate has AIDS and I'm not sleeping well."

SAUL *(To* DEALER 1) I'm not sleeping well.

DEALER 1 I have just the thing. Step right into my office.

DEALER 3 Speed, acid, mesc, ups, downs, 'ludes . . .

SAUL I'll take one hundred.

DEALER 1 Two dollars a cap.

RICH Forty's enough.

SAUL I wanted enough for both of us.

DEALER 1 You got the cash, I got the stash.

RICH Tristan and Isolde.

DEALER 1 Hey, man, you want them or not?

SAUL You don't understand anything!

DEALER 1 Look, man, I can't handle all that emotiating.

SAUL *(Near the breaking point)* You've never understood anything!

DEALER 1 Gimme the greens, I'll give you the reds.

RICH The widow throws herself on her husband's funeral pyre.

SAUL *(Hitting the bed with his fists. If* RICH *were the bed he'd be dead)* SHIT! SHIT! SHIT! You selfish bastard!

RICH What stopped you?

SAUL From hitting you?

RICH From buying the pills.

SAUL The pills? Nothing stopped me. I bought them.

RICH Thank you. Where are they?

SAUL I threw them away.

RICH Why?

SAUL Let me help you live!

RICH What's so hot about living when you're covered with lesions and you're coming down with a new infection every day? . . . If it gets too bad, I want to be able to quietly disappear.

SAUL I won't argue the logic of it. I can't do what you want me to do.

RICH I just want them around. You keep them for me—just in case.

SAUL I won't.

RICH Then I'll get them myself. I'll go out of here and get them.

(He climbs out of bed. He's shaky)

SAUL You're crazy.

RICH I don't need you to do my dirty work. *(He takes a few steps)* Where're my clothes? Where'd they put them?

SAUL Get back in bed!

RICH I want to get out of here! *(He puts on his robe)* This place is a death machine!

(He starts to leave but collapses on the floor)

SAUL *(Rushing to his aid)* You idiot.

RICH *(Catching his breath)* Well, here we are again. (SAUL *tries to help him back to bed)* No. Let me sit . . . Fuck . . . *(He sits in the chair)* "Dependent": from the Late Latin, "to hang from."

SAUL I tried to do what you asked me to do. Just like always.

RICH You don't have to apologize.

SAUL I want you to understand something.

RICH I understand.

SAUL It's important. Listen. I had made up my mind to give you half of the pills and keep the other half for myself. I was walking past Sheridan Square. It was starting to drizzle again. You've never seen Sheridan Square look grungier: a drunk was pissing on the pathetic little flowers. And that crazy lady—you know the one that sings off-key at the top of her lungs?—she was there, too. And my favorite, the guy with his stomach out to here—

RICH I get the picture.

SAUL There I was walking with the pills in my pocket, contemplating our suicides. And I was getting wet and cold. As I passed the square, Seconal seemed too slow to me. You don't have a monopoly on pain.

RICH I never thought—

SAUL Shut up. Anyway, I had stopped in front of the Pleasure Chest. I looked up and there in the window were sex toys and multicolored jockstraps, lit by a red neon sign. I said, "Help me, God." Which is funny coming from an atheist, let me tell you . . . I said it out loud.

RICH And you could walk again.

SAUL Well, it wasn't exactly a miracle, that's for sure.

RICH Thank God.

SAUL Anyway, there I was in front of a sex shop, and I looked down and there was a puddle. Now this'll sound stupid.

RICH Couldn't sound stupider than the rest.

SAUL In this dirty little puddle was a reflection of the red neon sign. It was beautiful. And the whole street was shining with the most incredible colors. They kept changing as the different signs blinked on and off . . . I don't know how long I stood there. A phrase came to my head: "The Lord taketh and the Lord giveth."

RICH You blew your punch line.

SAUL It's the other way around. Anyway, there went two hundred bucks down the sewer.

RICH Take it off your taxes.

SAUL Don't you see, I just don't have the right to take your life or mine.

RICH The Miracle of the Pleasure Chest.

SAUL Hang in there, Rich.

RICH Our Lady of Christopher Street.

SAUL Maybe I'm being selfish, but I want you here. I need you.

RICH My future isn't exactly promising.

SAUL I'll take you as is.

RICH But what happens when it gets worse? It's gonna get worse.

SAUL I'll be here for you no matter what happens.

RICH Will you?

SAUL I promise.

RICH Shit.

SAUL What do you want me to say?

RICH You're so goddamned noble.

SAUL How do you want me to be?

RICH I can't afford to be noble. The only thing holding me together is rage. It's not fair! Why me?

SAUL Why *not* you? Maybe it's me next. No one knows.

RICH I reserve the right to put an end to all this shit.

SAUL All right, but if you kill yourself they won't bury you in hallowed ground and you'll go to hell with all us Jews.

RICH I bet they have a separate AIDS section in the cemetery so I don't infect the other corpses. *(Beat, then suddenly he speaks fiercely)* Do you promise to stick with me no matter what happens?

SAUL I do.

RICH *Do you? (He searches* SAUL*'s face for the answer)* I need you. *(Long silence. He releases* SAUL) Paradise in a puddle.

SAUL You couldn't resist that, could you?

RICH Prodigies and signs, why not? It's the end of an era.

SAUL What do you think'll come next?

RICH Next? After I'm gone?

SAUL Don't be maudlin. You know I didn't mean that.

RICH I know you didn't . . . I've been wondering what happens after I die . . . Do you think things go on and on? I don't know. Is this all the time I have? I hope not . . . Do you think anywhere out there is a place as sweet as this one? I like it here—even though right now I am going through a lot of . . . *(He searches for the word)* difficulty . . . *(He goes back to bed)* And if we get to come back, where do we get to come back to?

I don't feature leaving here and going to a goddamned naphtha swamp in the Z sector of some provincial galaxy to live as some kind of weird insect . . . But if life is a kind of educational process in which each piece of the universe eventually gets to discover its own true divine nature, if it is, then a methane bog on Jupiter might serve just as well as a meadow in the Berkshires . . .

I want to be cremated and I want my ashes to fertilize the apple tree in the middle of Jake's pasture. When you take a bite of an apple from that tree you can think of me.

SAUL You'd be the worm in it.

RICH Saul?

SAUL What, Rich?

RICH There's a coffee shop way over by Tompkins Park, off of B. It holds maybe ten tables and has the scuzziest art on the walls.

SAUL What about it?

RICH I want to read my work there.

SAUL You turned down the Y.

RICH People go there, gay, straight, with their weird hair and their ears pierced ninety-nine different ways, they go there late in the evening, and there's a guitarist, and they sit there politely and listen. They look newborn, but slightly depraved. I want to read there when I get out of here. And you'll take pictures. Okay?

SAUL Sounds okay. Sounds good to me.

RICH Forgive me for being such a fuck.

SAUL You really are a fuck.

RICH I'm a real prick.

SAUL You're an asshole.

RICH You're a faggot.

SAUL You're a fruit.

RICH You know, if we took precautions . . .

SAUL If what? What? You always do that.

RICH I don't know.

SAUL Would you like to?

RICH If we're careful. Do you want to?

SAUL I'd love to. What do you think?

RICH I think it'd be okay.

SAUL What'll we do?

RICH I don't know. Something safe.

SAUL We'll think of something.

RICH Close the curtain.

SAUL Do you think we should?

RICH Well, we can't do it like this.

SAUL Right.

RICH Right.

SAUL What if someone comes in?

RICH So what?

SAUL Right.
(SAUL *doesn't move)*

RICH So what are you waiting for?

SAUL I'm scared.

RICH So am I. Do you think we should?

SAUL God, I want to.

RICH Well, close the fucking curtain! *(The* HOSPICE WORKER *ends the impasse by closing the curtain)* Thanks.

SAUL Thanks.
(When the curtain is completely shut, the HOSPICE WORKER *walks downstage center)*

HOSPICE WORKER I have a new AIDS patient, Richard. He still has a lot of denial about his condition. Which is normal. I think most of us would go crazy if we had to face our own deaths squarely. He's a wonderful man. He writes extraordinarily funny poems about the ward. His lover's there all the time, and he's got a lot of friends visiting, and both families. I only hope it keeps up. It's only his second time in the hospital. They get a lot of support at first, but as the illness goes on, the visitors stop coming—and they're left with only me.

But something tells me it's not going to happen in his case. You should see how his lover takes care of him. God forbid they treat Rich badly, Saul swoops down and lets them have it. He's making a real pain in the ass of himself, which is sometimes how you have to be in this situation.

Rich will be out of the hospital again in a week or so. For a while. He's a fighter . . . The angry phase is just about over and the bargaining phase is beginning. If he behaves like a good little boy, God will do what Rich tells Him to do . . . I certainly hope that God does.

I don't know anymore. Sometimes I think I'm an atheist. No. Not really. It's more that I'm angry at God: how can He do this? *(Pause) I* have a lot of denial, *I* am angry, and *I* bargain with God. I have a long way to go towards acceptance. Maybe it's time for me to resign. Maybe I'm suffering from burnout.

But what would I do if I didn't go there? And it's a privilege to be with people when they are dying. Sometimes they tell you the most amazing things. The other night Jean-Jacques—he's this real queen, there's no other word for it—he told me what he misses most in the hospital is his corset and high heels. I mean he weighs all of ninety pounds and he's half-dead. But I admire his spirit. The way they treat him. Sometimes they won't even bring the food to his bed. And I'm afraid to complain for fear they take it out on him! Damn them! . . . I've lost some of my idealism, as I said. Last night I painted his nails for him. *(She shows the audience her vividly painted fingernails)* Flaming red. He loved it.

End of Play

About the Author

William M. Hoffman, a native New Yorker, started writing for the theater at the legendary Off-Off-Broadway showcase the Caffe Cino. He is a member of the Circle Repertory Company but has also worked at La Mama, Playwrights Horizons, and the Manhattan Theater Club. He is co-author (with Anthony Holland) of three comedies, *Cornbury, Shoe Palace Murray,* and *The Cherry Orchard, Part Two,* and wrote the book and co-wrote the lyrics (with composer John Braden) to the musicals *Gulliver's Travels* and *Etiquette.* In recognition of his work, Hoffman has received Guggenheim and New York Foundation for the Arts fellowships and two National Endowment for the Arts grants. He has written for both big and small screens and is the editor of four play anthologies, including *Gay Plays.* He is currently completing the libretto for an opera entitled *A Figaro for Antonia* (music by John Corigliano), commissioned by the Metropolitan Opera in honor of its hundredth anniversary.

As Is received the 1985 Drama Desk Award for Outstanding New Play, an Obie Award for Distinguished Playwriting, and three Tony nominations, including Best Play.